T0328524

VIJAYA DHARMA SŪRI

SHASTRA-VISHARADA JAIN ACHARYA
SHRI VIJAYA DHARMA SURI

Jain Literature Society

VIJAYA DHARMA SŪRI

HIS LIFE AND WORK

BY

A. J. SUNAVALA, B.A., LL.B.

WITH A PREFATORY NOTE BY
F. W. THOMAS

CAMBRIDGE
AT THE UNIVERSITY PRESS
1922

CAMBRIDGE
UNIVERSITY PRESS

University Printing House, Cambridge CB2 8BS, United Kingdom

Cambridge University Press is part of the University of Cambridge.

It furthers the University's mission by disseminating knowledge in the pursuit of
education, learning and research at the highest international levels of excellence.

www.cambridge.org
Information on this title: www.cambridge.org/9781316612750

© Cambridge University Press 1922

First published 1922
First paperback edition 2016

A catalogue record for this publication is available from the British Library

ISBN 978-1-316-61275-0 Paperback

PREFATORY NOTE

THE subject of this interesting memoir holds a position of great distinction and influence among the Jain community; and the reader will himself have the feeling of being in contact with a man of original force and character. But a few words may still help us in appreciating the significance of Vijaya Dharma Sūri's work.

There are not a few Jain *Sādhus* in India, presiding over their large or small communities, instructing and edifying their disciples, studying their canonical texts, publishing editions of them or original works relating to them. Such pious and learned men have never been wanting among the Jains. Nor has there been a lack of loyal supporters who have liberally contributed what was desirable for the erection and maintenance of shrines and institutions or for literary enterprise. The practice of the community, which encourages a gradual assimilation of the laity to its ascetic leaders and which accords to the Sheth, or influential layman, a recognized position, has in this respect borne abundant fruit. But an inquirer would probably find that at the present time the cultivation and support of literary enterprise is unusually active among the Jains; and he would hardly be mistaken in attributing this in a large measure to the example of Vijaya Dharma Sūri.

Apart from the purely personal qualities depicted in the memoir, the singular force of character, and sincerity of conviction, the dignified, unaffected mildness and friendliness, which characterize the saint, we shall, no doubt, be right in selecting his openmindedness and wideness of outlook as his most distinctive traits. Not only have his activities been, as shown in the memoir, of a many-sided character, but he has extended a cordial welcome to western personalities and methods, facilitating in many ways the work of scholars and himself complying with their critical principles. In this way he has come to be regarded as the true mediator between Jain thought and the west; while his own literary labours have been recognized in the highest quarters by election to honorary membership of societies and by grants of titles of distinction. This does not at all imply an abatement of faith in his own religion: on the contrary, the serenity of his assurance is the real basis of his receptivity. Himself an unsparing observer of the rules of his order, he is free from pedantry in his demands upon others; and, while exercising a remarkable and far-reaching authority, he will be found rather pleading and reasoning with his disciples and friends than laying down the law. No wonder if similar graces reappear conspicuously among his devoted followers.

The Jain doctrine and community are ancient, having an unbroken continuity from an early period of Indian religious thought. They are marked by

rationality and consistency of principle, ethical outlook, and ascetic practice. In the present period of
transition such traits are a strong equipment: the
qualities of representative leaders such as Vijaya
Dharma Sūri will contribute to a further expansion
of the community.

The author has not laboured to include every
interesting particular in the life of the teacher—it was
not his purpose to do so. A reader anxious to learn
more may find something to his purpose in the
accounts mentioned at the end of Chapter II and also
in the late Dr. L. P. Tessitori's *Vijaya Dharma Suri:
A Jain Āchārya of the Present Day* (*Calcutta*, 1917).

F. W. THOMAS.

April, 1921.

CONTENTS

		PAGE
I.	INTRODUCTORY	11
II.	GENERAL CONSIDERATIONS . . .	17
III.	BIRTH AND EARLY YEARS . . .	23
IV.	RENUNCIATION	26
V.	PREPARATION FOR A GREAT MISSION .	31
VI.	COMMENCEMENT OF A TRIUMPHAL TOUR	34
VII.	THE YASHOVIJAYA JAINA PĀTHASHĀLĀ AT BENARES	38
VIII.	THE MONK AT THE COURT OF THE MAHĀRĀJA OF BENARES . .	42
IX.	THE SANĀTANA DHARMA MAHĀSABHĀ AT ALLAHABAD AND THE PILGRIMAGE TO THE JAIN TĪRTHAS OF BIHĀR .	45
X.	MISSION IN BENGAL	48
XI.	CONSECRATION OF MONKS . . .	52
XII.	SHĀTRAVISHĀRADA JAINĀCHĀRYA .	55
XIII.	THE JAIN ĀCHĀRYA AND WESTERN SCHOLARS	58
XIV.	JAINISM, ANCIENT AND MODERN. REVIVAL OF JAIN LEARNING AND CULTURE—THE END AND THE MEANS	64

B

PAGE

XV. THE LIFE OF THE MONK AND ITS
LESSONS 68

XVI. VIJAYA DHARMA SŪRI AS A MONK,
A SCHOLAR AND A PREACHER . 71

XVII. LITERARY ACTIVITY AND ITS RESULTS 76

XVIII. CONCLUSION—AN IDEAL MONK . . 81

VIJAYA DHARMA SŪRI:
HIS LIFE AND WORK

I

INTRODUCTORY

To those who are interested only in the passing
concerns of the moment, whose sole object of care and
study is the accumulation of wealth, or the acquisition
of power and authority, rank and renown, who bestow
not a single thought upon the perpetual concerns of
life, or upon the profound problems of the spiritual
existence, which always and ever attract the attention
of the highest mind of man, that holy teaching of
Jesus Christ: 'Take no thought, saying, What shall
we eat? or, What shall we drink? or, Wherewithal
shall we be clothed?', 'Seek ye first the kingdom of
God and His righteousness; and all these things shall
be added unto you,' this holiest of holy teachings may
seem to have no meaning, and appear as the teaching
of a dreaming enthusiast, an unpractical visionary.
To them it seems that the sermon of the Christian
Prophet takes no account of the realities of this earthly
life and the daily necessities of this world, and has,
therefore, no bearing on the conduct of an individual,
or that of a community or a nation.

HISTORY AND ITS LESSONS

If, however, we examine this teaching by the light
of the lessons which History instils—and History
is in such matters our surest and safest guide—if
we examine it by the help of those lives which
form the soul of all good biographies, we shall find
that a nation's greatness, a nation's power, peace and
prosperity have resulted from, and have always
depended upon, not men of selfish ends and interests, not men who lived contented with earning
their own bread and seeking their own happiness,
not men who pursued their own pleasures and sought
the gratification of their own wants and desires,
regarding themselves as the centre of all their thoughts
and actions, but those noble and selfless characters
who thought less of themselves and more of others,
who devoted their talents, their energies and their
lives to the service of their country and their people,
who loved the land of their birth, the glory and
the renown of their race, with so pure an affection
that they counted it a joy and an honour beyond
price to work and even to suffer for their sake.
Take away these characters and their deeds from the
pages of History, and see then what remains of
History at all? History then becomes a perfect blank.
It has little to tell; still less to teach. And, if
countries that have become great and prosperous
owe their greatness and their prosperity to the self-
denying labours of the men who lived and worked

for them, who used their reason and their capacities for the elevation and regeneration of mankind in general and their own people in particular, is not theirs the character which ought to be built and developed by every man in himself? is not theirs the example which ought to enliven his spirit and illuminate his soul? is not theirs the life and career which ought to animate his ambitions and aspirations, rouse his energies and emotions?

MEN WE WANT AND WORSHIP

These are the lives we admire and esteem; these are the lives we revere and worship. These are the men we love and require; not men who are selfish triflers, interested calculators who think only of personal gain and personal loss. We want men whose first question is 'what good can I *do*?' and not 'what good can I *gain*?' We want men who are self-denying and self-sacrificing,—men worthy to be called men and hence worthy of our respect. We want men who will be constantly watching for an opportunity to serve their fellow-men, and are ready to trample under their feet their selfishness, their own personal interests, when they come in conflict with the general good. We want men who will regard every contact with another man as an opportunity of being useful to him in some way or other, and are prepared to put aside all puerile questions of race, caste and creed, as they put away a soiled cloth, or a worn-out garment, for the enlightenment and happiness of mankind.

We want men who will labour not only for the present
generation, but also for the next and the succeeding
ones ; men who, seeing the miserable state of the religious world,—seeing the noble and sacred faiths debased,
the old and solemn rites and observances ridiculed
and derided, the temples, the churches, the mosques,
and the holy shrines thronged by hypocrites and
mockers—burn with a desire to rekindle the fires of
morality and spirituality upon the defiled and polluted
altars, and bring back the knowledge and the wisdom
of the ancient *Gurus* and *Rishis* within the reach of
a sin-burdened world.   The lives of such men will be
a constant source of inspiration to those who are in
the ditch of darkness, ever struggling against the
storms of life, sometimes discouraged, sometimes dis-
heartened over seeming failures, and even at times
ready to give up the battle.   The records of such
careers will beckon the fallen to awake, to arise and
forge forward in the fight of life, and will inspire both
the young and the old to transmute their very failures
into success.

LIFE, ITS END AND OBJECT

Life, it has been truly observed, is Duty, and it
seems that all worldly wisdom of the highest character
is summed up by the poet in his two expressive lines

‘ I slept and dreamt that life was Beauty—
I woke and found that life was Duty.’

Life is, indeed, Duty, which means doing.   There is
a high purpose in it—something serious about it.   It

is not given to man that it may be wasted, or that it may be frittered away or trifled with. It is to manifest in full glory and activity the Power, the Wisdom and the Love that are its birthright. It is to become perfect, as perfect as the 'Father in Heaven is Perfect.' Herein lies the true and rational solution of the great problem of life, one in which Science and Religion and Philosophy find their proper place and function, and are all welded together into one harmonious and magnificent whole.

THE LAW OF SELF-SACRIFICE THE LAW OF DEVELOPMENT FOR MAN

But, in order to reach this highest state, the state of perfection, the craving of selfishness should be first destroyed. Everything that is selfish, everything that is personal, everything that is of the lower nature must be burnt up before the goal is reached and attained. Hard, hard it is for man to get rid of selfishness; for, in doing so, he has to conquer a habit which he took years and ages in forming. This personal element of selfishness had its use and its place in those earlier stages; as one of the Masters of Wisdom once put it: 'The law of the survival of the fittest is the law of evolution for the brute; but the law of intelligent self-sacrifice is the law of development for man.' So it comes that man needs to transcend what was formerly his own nature and to build into himself the excellent virtue of unselfishness, in order that he may learn to sacrifice what seems his personal interest for the good of humanity as a whole. A man whose conception of life is high realizes the value of this lesson in its entirety. He realizes that life is given to him that he may do something that will endure; and nothing endures so much as a good deed done for the public good. He lives that others may live. He regards himself as one to whom life has been given that he may serve others and make them happy. He realizes that he is born, not for himself solely, but for others—not only for his family, but also for his country. And, realizing this his real duty in life, he discharges it with courage and self-reliance, serving humanity, without expecting others to do that service for himself. Such a career, indeed, becomes a vast subject of reflection. Such is the career of Vijaya Dharma Sūri, whose life and work it is the object of these pages to describe.

II

GENERAL CONSIDERATIONS

THE ANCIENT ORDER OF MONKS

THE *Āchārya* whose life it is here proposed to sketch belongs to the most ancient and sacred Order of Monks, whose bond of union is not the acceptance or profession of a common belief, but a common search and a common aspiration for Truth—Truth which forms the basis of all religions, and which cannot be claimed as the exclusive possession of any. He belongs to those monks who regard Truth as a prize to be striven for, not as a dogma to be imposed by authority; who maintain that Truth should be sought by study and reflection, by contemplation and meditation, by purity of life and conduct, by consecration and devotion to high ideals; who hold that religious belief should be the result of individual study or intuition, and not its antecedent, and should rest on knowledge, not on assertion; who illuminate the scriptures, and explain and elucidate the doctrines and tenets of religions, by unveiling their hidden meanings, thus justifying them at the bar of intellectual criticism, as they are ever justified in the eyes of intuition; who consider every religion as an expression of the Ancient Wisdom, and prefer its study to its condemnation, and its practice to proselytism; who extend tolerance to all, even to the intolerant, not as a privi-

lege to bestow, but as a duty to perform, ever seeking
to remove ignorance, not to punish it ; who endeavour
to restore to the world the Science of the Spirit,
asking man to realize the Self, the true Self, the God
within, teaching him to know the Spirit, the *Ātman*,
as himself, and the mind and body as his servants.

THEIR BENEFICENT WORK FOR HUMANITY

These are the monks, who have been continuously
carrying on their beneficent work for humanity,
pouring down from their lofty heights freely and
abundantly high and noble ideals, sublime and inspiring thoughts, pure and devotional aspirations,
streams of intellectual and spiritual help for mankind.
These are the self-denying, selfless souls, who have
completely and unconditionally dedicated themselves
to the service of humanity, bending all the sublime
powers that they hold to the quickening of the evolution of the human race. With all the mighty forces at
their command, they devote themselves freely and
fully to the cultivation of spiritual knowledge, spiritual
wisdom and spiritual aspiration, weaning people from
their sole and supreme devotion to the objects of the
senses, pointing out to them the path of spiritual progress, which will necessarily render them less likely
to sacrifice the higher dictates of humanity on the
altars of their individual earthly interests, guiding
them into those paths of purity and holiness, which
will ultimately lead them to the vast ocean of spiritual consciousness, wherein alone can be found pure

life, pure thought and pure joy,—the true *Sat-Chit-Ānanda* of existence.

GREAT SERVICES RENDERED BY VIJAYA DHARMA SŪRI

Futile, indeed, it would be to enumerate the great services, which Vijaya Dharma Sūri, the distinguished Monk, has rendered to humanity in general, and his own people in particular. His extraordinary activity, eloquence and power of persuasion, which have resulted in the creation of a number of educational and philanthropical institutions, such as schools, printing-presses, libraries, hospitals and *āshramas*; his learning, scholarship and sound erudition, which have resulted in the issuing of journals and periodicals, in the publication of an important part of the Jain literature which had hitherto remained ignored, and in the dissemination of a correct knowledge of the principles and tenets of the Jain religion; his interest in the productions of the ancient Jain civilization, such as stone inscriptions and manuscripts—the relics of a glorious past—which the apathy and ignorance of the people had allowed to decay and rot in neglect, and his efforts to preserve and divulge the same; his crusade against the killing of animals, and his battles so earnestly fought in favour of righteousness and renunciation; his self-devotion and self-sacrifice in the interest of all that is good and virtuous; his tolerance of, and broad sympathy with, men of all castes and creeds, and his unbounded selfless love for humanity—all these explain the cause of his world-wide fame, all these have combined to make him the most noteworthy figure of the present day.

INTELLECTUAL AND MORAL GREATNESS

Much more might be said in marking general and popular features. Mental characteristics might be traced in his eager, ardent and sympathetic ear, in his kind, tender and expressive eye, his sweet, marvellous and melodious voice, his keen intellect, his penetrating insight, his presence the embodiment of stateliness and dignity. We pass over in silence his inner life of religion; we pass over in silence his quiet deeds of reclamation and philanthropy. Observe, however, that it is not the qualities or attributes enumerated here, singly or in combination, that have ennobled Vijaya Dharma Sūri, and enthroned him in his citadel of human hearts. His is less an intellectual than a moral greatness and power. What men admire, adore and revere is *himself*—the great and singular and wonderful personality: a scholar of academic refinement in sympathy with the people and their needs; a monk combining in himself the strictest observance of the monastic vows with a liberal interpretation of the spirit of his religion; a sage of clear and far extending vision, at once patient, prompt and enthusiastic; in character lofty, yet humble and unassuming; of disciplined self-control combined with energy and earnestness; of a strength of will that has never quailed before mind or multitude, accumulated wealth or regal power and pomp, that has never failed in the darker and deeper trials of malice, jealousy or envenomed hate; of moral powers that shine the brighter in the gloom of party spirit and party strife, caste feelings and caste jealousies, sectarian dislikes and disputes, religious contests, quarrels and controversies.

A LEADER IN THE RANKS OF THOUGHT

Passing from personal characteristics to his services in the domain of learning and literature, we find that Vijaya Dharma Sūri rightly deserves to be called a leader in the ranks of thought. His spiritual culture, which is abundantly evidenced by the huge mass of works written and published by him, is admittedly of the highest order. In recognition of his great services in the sphere of literature and his valuable contributions to the domain of thought, he has been honoured by the distinguished title of *Shāstravishārada Jaināchārya*, conferred on him by the consensus of a large number of Pandits from all parts of India. Again, he has had the honour of having been elected as an Associate Member of the Asiatic Society of Bengal. He is also very well known to all orientalists in Europe whose sphere of work is directly or indirectly associated with Jainism. It is rather strange that his literary talents should have thus far received inadequate attention from Indian scholars. It is, indeed, a matter of regret that the literary merits of the great Monk should not have been so widely known and extensively recognized in India, the land of his own birth, as they have been known and recognized in Europe amongst the circle of Jainologists and other Sanskrit and Prākrit scholars.   It will be a cause of not a little surprise to people in India to know that the Western scholars have evinced a great deal of interest in the life and work of the *Āchārya,* so much so that some of them, e. g. Dr. J. Hertel of Germany, Dr. A. Guérinot of France, and Dr. F. Belloni-Filippi of Italy have written biographical accounts of him in scientific Oriental Journals.

III

BIRTH AND EARLY YEARS

PARENTAGE, TIME AND PLACE OF BIRTH

In any review of the life of a great man, and in appreciation of his achievements, we naturally tend to look at the beginning of his career, and see what chances he had in life and what he made of them. We see some men born in easy circumstances, who have never had an opportunity of toiling or labouring, who have never known from close daily contact what human suffering means, rich and prosperous, and have drifted, as naturally as a river flows, into lives of benevolence and usefulness; while there are others, who start from humble beginnings, and with a daily struggle for existence, with no means and opportunities at their command, with no advantages of birth or favour or fortune, and yet in spite of these obstacles, undismayed by embarrassment or difficulty, undisturbed by clamour or confusion, undaunted by intricacy or perplexity, undeterred by obloquy or opposition, fight valiantly and courageously what they call the battle of life, developing day after day the seeds of virtue and of goodness that are lying latent within them, ultimately achieving a moral and a spiritual triumph—the true greatness—in the end. And Vijaya Dharma Sūri belonged to the latter class.

Sprung from a humble *Vaishya* family of the *Visā Shrīmālī* clan, he was born at Mahuwā in Kathiawar, in the year 1868. The father, Rāma Chandra, and the mother, Kamlā Dēvī, called the child Mūla Chandra. He soon became the joy of his parents and friends. There appears to have been nothing extraordinary in his early career, except that he grew up like a child of the streets, apparently in ignorance of his high destiny. As we trace the life which he led as a boy, as a youth, down to the date when he assumed the garb of a monk, we find him leading a purely thought-less life,—a life that did not recognize its own great-ness, with the mind not yet realizing its mission, nor the part it had to play. He was sent to the village school along with other boys of his class and age, and among these he soon distinguished himself very highly in various forms of physical exercise and field games. In his studies properly so called, however, he failed to give his teacher and parents satisfaction or promise of any kind, being habitually irregular in attendance and inattentive to his lessons. The schoolmaster gave him up in despair, and the father at last took the boy, when he was only ten years old, into his shop, thinking that he would help him in his daily work.

GAMBLING HIS ONLY INTEREST

Mūla Chandra, however, would neither learn nor earn. His only interest was in gambling and specu-lation, which were the predominant vices of the time, and to which he had become very strongly addicted,

even in his early years. Instead of in any way helping the old father in his business, he squandered his
money in gambling. In vain did the parents try to
persuade their beloved son to desist from the evil
course ; in vain did they beseech him to refrain from
indulging in this most odious and debasing vice ; in
vain did they warn him against the perilous and
ruinous course,—the course of constant anxiety, constant apprehension and general gloom — a course
utterly destructive of all human happiness. He disregarded all their prayers, he disregarded all their
entreaties, all their commands. But, inasmuch as ' the
Furies are the bonds of men ', and the poisons are
often-times the principal medicines, which kill the
disease and save the life, so this vice of gambling
proved, in fact, a blessing in disguise, and eventually
led to his salvation.

D

IV

RENUNCIATION

CIRCUMSTANCES LEADING TO RENUNCIATION

ONE day Mūla Chandra lost a large amount of money in gambling, and was, in consequence, severely taken to task by his parents. It was then that he began to think of the vanity of possession, the instability of wealth, the fickleness of fortune, and the greed for money which had caused him to displease his parents, and his parents to punish him. By defeat, by humiliation, by loss of sympathy and support, he came to learn a wider truth and humanity than before. For now comes the moment when, for the first time, he says to himself, ' I have had enough of all this; I no longer care for money or wealth—it ends in sorrow and disappointment; I no longer care for riches, opulence, or affluence—they are a burden rather than a joy; I no longer care for the things that break in the enjoyment; I no longer care for the things that perish in the using.' And then sets in that dissatisfaction, that divine discontent with the fleeting and the transitory goods of this earth; that which the Shāstras call *Vairāgya*—dispassion, freedom from passion. He becomes indifferent to earthly objects. These objects have no power over him; they no longer attract him; they have lost their attractive power.

These objects of the senses, as it is said in the *Gītā*, the Song of the Lord, turn away from the abstemious dweller in the body.

IN SEARCH OF A GURU

Being in this manner dissatisfied with the world and its objects, Mūla Chandra soon began to feel that the household life was full of hindrance, the haunt of passion, and that the homeless state—the life of seclusion—was the life of bliss. His uneasiness began to increase day after day, and his resolve to live the spiritual life grew stronger and stronger, until at last the time came when he made up his mind to renounce; and one day, without informing any one where he was going, he definitely abandoned his paternal house, and went forth alone, homeless, in search of a *Guru*, a preceptor, who would give him the happiness, the eternal and everlasting peace and happiness, which he was longing for.

VRIDDHI CHANDRA AND HIS SERMON

Leaving Mahuwā, Mūla Chandra went to Bhawnagar, where the venerable monk, Vriddhi Chandra, was living. Vriddhi Chandra was a great preacher, known for his high degree of learning and piety. His absolute unselfishness and meekness of character had ensured for him the love of his followers and the respect even of those who differed from his views. His sermons as well as the private discourses and disputations which he was holding with orthodox and heterodox visitors in the *Upāshraya* were deeply en-

gaging the attention and interest of the people. One
day Mūla Chandra went into the *Upāshraya* and sat
at the feet of the holy hermit, listening to the dis-
course, which had for its subject the following verse :—

मृत्योर्बिभेषि किं मूढ ! भीतं मुञ्चति नो यमः ।
अजातं नैव गृह्णाति कुरु यत्नमजन्मनि ॥ १ ॥

'*Why do you fear Death, O Fool ?* (For) *Yama* (the
God of Death) *does not let go the frightened man.
He never catches hold of the unborn;* (therefore) *en-
deavour not to be born.*'

WHAT BINDS MAN TO RE-BIRTH IS DESIRE

In this sermon the great sage beseeches the people
to cast away every sort of attachment that binds man
to re-birth. For that which draws man to re-birth in
this world is *desire*; the desire to obtain and enjoy
the things that here may be obtained and enjoyed, the
desire to possess and achieve the things that here may
be possessed and achieved. Every man who sets
before him some earthly aim, every man who makes
the goal of his life some earthly object or ambition,
that man is evidently bound by desire; and, so long as
he desires that which the earth can give him, he must
return for it; so long as any joy or any object belong-
ing to the transitory life is a thing that has power to
attract, that has power to tempt, it is a thing that has
also power to bind, power to hold and constrain. It
is the *desire* that ties or enchains the soul to re-birth,
and therefore it is written that only when ' the bonds
of the heart are broken ' can the soul reach liberation.

FINAL INITIATION

Mūla Chandra, whose eyes were now fully opened to the evils of the unprofitable life that he had hitherto led, was deeply impressed by the serenity and majesty of the monk's holy appearance, and learnt from his sermon the true solution of the problem of life and a remedy for the miseries of this world. At the end of the sermon he approached the worthy sage, and manifested to him his desire to be initiated as a monk ; for he realized that here at least was one who rose superior to the otherwise universal ills of life. The prudent sage, however, considering the immaturity of the applicant, and the failings which are incident to youth and inexperience, refused to grant his request, and advised him to go back to his parents and obtain their consent. The task was by no means an easy one ; for the boy was the darling of his parents, and, what was more, their youngest son. But Mūla Chandra had already taken an aversion to the world ; the voice of his real vocation had already spoken to him ; and, though some days were still to elapse before his initiation as a monk, yet he had already made his resolution, and every day that passed made him firmer and firmer in it.

He went back to Mahuwā, and requested his parents to give him the required permission. But the parents were greatly disappointed. They begged, they blamed, they remonstrated. They expressed their displeasure, their disapprobation, and urged reasons in opposition. But Mūla Chandra was firm. He had formed within himself a resolution to renounce the world—a resolution which no earthly circumstances could change or alter. He overcame all the objections raised by his father and soothed the tears of his loving mother, who bewailed her sad fate. At last, having with great difficulty obtained their consent, he came back to Bhawnagar, and, throwing himself at the feet of the *Guru*, begged to be invested with the garb of the monk. Satisfied with the earnestness and enthusiasm of the youth, Vṛiddhi Chandra received him with pleasure; and, having made him go through the formalities needed, initiated him into the holy Order of Monks. Thus, in his nineteenth year, on the 12th day of May, 1887, Mūla Chandra was consecrated a monk, to be known from that time by the name of *Dharma Vijaya*.

V

PREPARATION FOR A GREAT MISSION

THE LIFE-STORY OF A MONK BEGINS WITH HIS DĪKSHĀ

THE life-story of a monk or an ascetic may be said really to begin with his initiation or *Dīkshā*. For, if one reads the lives and biographies of the great Jaina sages, he will be convinced that the Jainas did not intend their monks to enclose themselves within the narrow circle of their monasteries, in the performance of the innumerable religious duties, and in the company of a few devout lay adherents. The life of the monk is not to be only one of absolute detachment, to be spent in study and in meditation; he is also expected to preach to the people, to give them advice and admonition, to become at once their teacher and their leader, their guide and their *Guru*. The task is, no doubt, beset with difficulties. To be a great religious teacher in the East is not the same thing as to be the head of some great faith in the West. For in the East the religious teacher, while observing the most absolute purity and devoting his whole life to the highest spirituality, never touches money in any shape or form. The first rule of his life is that he must possess no earthly things whatever, excepting the garb that he wears, and even this garb is so made as to be valueless for sale.

HIS STUDIES

So far Dharma Vijaya had had no opportunity to develop the seeds of his real vocation, which were lurking in the fertile, but uncultivated, soil of his mind. His intelligence was not dull, it was only dormant; and now the course of discipline and instruction ordained by the Brotherhood of Monks, the strictest observance of the monastic vows, prayers and penances, study and disputations, all combined to bring his vigorous dialectical and logical powers to the front. Stimulated by the example of his *Guru*, and under his kind and able guidance, Dharma Vijaya began to study the *Pratikramaṇa Sūtra*, learned grammar and mastered the *Sārasvata Chandrikā*. He then obtained initiation into the study of the Sanskrit and Prākrit literatures, and began to master the *Jaina Sūtras*, the canonical texts of the Jain religion.

DEATH OF THE GURU

Vṛiddhi Chandra was fully cognizant of the ability, intelligence and enthusiasm of his pupil and also of the great mental and moral capabilities that were latent in him. He watched with great satisfaction the marvellous progress of his young disciple. Unfortunately, he was not destined to live long, for he died in the year 1893, leaving behind him, among other disciples, his most esteemed pupil Dharma Vijaya. A nobler, a purer, a gentler, and a sweeter soul,—a soul more peaceful, more serene, and more constant in adversity—a soul more fitted by virtue, and chastity and self-denial to enter into the eternal peace, never passed into that world of perfection, that lofty region, where there is nothing but perfect joy, perfect bliss, and perfect wisdom. And his disciples, who were now left alone, never felt themselves so hopeful and so encouraged as from the glorious sense of possibility which was inspired by the memory of one who, in the midst of difficulties of every kind, and breathing an atmosphere heavy with corruption, yet showed himself so wise, so good, and so great a man. Of him it may be truly said :

> ' O framed for nobler times and calmer hearts !
> O studious thinker eloquent for truth !
> Philosopher, despising wealth and death,
> But patient, childlike, full of life and love ! '

VI

COMMENCEMENT OF A TRIUMPHAL TOUR

PANNYĀSA-PADA

SOME time before his death Vṛiddhi Chandra had recommended Dharma Vijaya for the *Pannyāsa-pada*, which gave him the first place among the disciples. And Dharma Vijaya was fully qualified to be the successor of his preceptor. His sermons had already engaged the attention and interest of the people; the fame of his discourses and disputations had already spread; the strength of his courage and convictions had already begun to be extensively known.

THE NET RESULT OF THE TOUR

Dharma Vijaya was now left without a guide, to be himself a guide to others. Ever since the day of his consecration as a monk he had made up his mind to become a preacher for the benefit of mankind. With this end in view, soon after his *Guru's* death, he left Bhawnagar, and, except for the *Chaturmāsa* of each year,—the four months of the rainy season, during which Jain monks are not allowed to peregrinate, he proceeded from place to place bare-headed and bare-footed, with no conveyance but his bare feet, with no luggage but his begging-bowl, with no guide but his faith. Endowed with knowledge and righteousness and austerity, vowed to perpetual poverty and chastity and truthfulness, possessing nothing and dependent for his very subsistence on the alms of the charitable, the homeless ascetic passed from one place to another, wandering through the villages, towns, and cities of Kathiawar, Gujarat, and Marwar, everywhere preaching and propagating his religion, everywhere conferring invaluable benefits upon mankind. We see him moving from place to place, living the life of a teacher, a life beautiful in its purity, simplicity and sincerity, radiant with love, with compassion, and with all the tenderest emotions of the human heart. We see him raising, by his power of speech and persuasion, the ignorant masses from their secular sluggishness, stimulating them to activity, and awakening in them an interest in all that is good and true and noble. We see him, by his eloquence and instruction, curing the illiterate and uneducated people of their gross superstitions, their petty jealousies, their social prejudices, and thus making them purer and happier, more peaceful and more contented. We see him, by his learning and exhortation and influence, presenting and spreading the truer and deeper views of his faith, composing religious disputes and differences, restoring and re-establishing the annual pilgrimages which had long been discontinued and left in neglect, thus causing the considerable wealth of the community to be spent in charitable institutions of public utility, and in this way infusing a new life into the decaying, but not dying, body of Jainism.

VISIT TO THE LAND OF HIS BIRTH

In the year 1900 Dharma Vijaya went to Mahuwā, the land which was his birthplace, and where he had never been since his consecration as a monk. When he arrived there, he found his father dead; but his mother, who was anxious to see her son, came, along with other people of the village, to meet him and to reverence him. As he entered the village with his monks and disciples, the mother's eager eyes naturally turned towards the object of her affection. She was exceedingly glad to behold her son after the lapse of so many years. She looked at him with mingled feelings of joy and sorrow, delight and despair. She beheld her son—the son who was the source of her joy and her happiness—bare-headed and bare-footed, in the garb of a begging monk. She beheld her beloved son—the son to whom she had given birth, but whom, she thought, she could no longer call her own—the son whom she could no longer receive in her own house, nor clasp in her own arms. And, when the people of the village saw the monk, as he walked slowly in the midst of his white-clad disciples, and joined their hands, and did homage to him, how many of them could have recognized in that monk of the serene face and saintly appearance, the naughty Mūla Chandra, the bad youth who used to sit in his father's shop and squander his father's money in gambling and speculation! Dharma Vijaya spent the *Chatur-māsa* of the year, the four months of the rainy season, in Mahuwā. He preached to the people, who admired his simple, but subtle and forcible eloquence. He exhorted them to ponder seriously over matters which affected their vital interests, their social and moral well-being. The example of his life was not without its effect and efficacy; for in Mahuwā he consecrated two new monks before his departure from that town.

VII

THE YASHOVIJAYA JAINA PĀTHASHĀLĀ AT BENARES

OPENING OF A SCHOOL AT MĀNDAL

THE wonderful activities of Dharma Vijaya, however, did not end here. He fully realized that the results produced and the objects achieved would not last long, if the efforts which had brought them about were not continued. The best means to secure a continuation of these efforts was, in his opinion, to found an institution where students would not only receive an education imbued with the philanthropic principles of Jainism, but, on leaving it after finishing the course of their study, would also carry with them those principles and spread the knowledge of the same over all parts of India. With this end in view, he opened at Māndal in Gujarat, in the year 1902, a school on a small scale, and called it the *Yashovijaya Jaina Pāthashālā*, after the name of the great Jain polygraph of the seventeenth century.

DEPARTURE FOR BENARES

It seemed, however, that an institution on the lines proposed could not prosper in a place like Māndal. He, therefore, thought it necessary to remove the College to a more central place, and selected for it

Benares—the traditional seat of Brahmanic learning, the heart of Hinduism. The idea was, perhaps, more plausible than practicable. It was considered almost impossible for a Jain *Sādhu* to cross the vast stretch of land bare-footed, and found a Jain College in a place where Jainism was almost unknown and people were determinedly hostile. Those who knew him tried to dissuade him from his intentions and earnestly besought him to desist, but nothing could shake Dharma Vijaya's *faith*. He remained unmoved, strong and steady in his resolution; for nothing that can happen to the manifested world can shake the sublime serenity and peacefulness of him who has risen to the realization of the *Self* of all. ' It is better to try nobly and to fail than ignobly not to try at all '; that, in fact, is the great inspiration for him who has caught a glimpse of the highest. His own intelligence directed him; his own conscience guided him. The consent of the intelligence, the consent of the conscience, these were the true strength of the hero. He had chosen his highest, and he desired to follow it unflinchingly. He knew his own strength; he knew his own endurance. He was ready for the stones that would pierce his feet; he was ready for the thorns that would tear his flesh. Confiding in his faith, and confiding in the goodness of his cause, he set out for Benares, accompanied by six monks and a dozen pupils; and, overcoming all the difficulties of the road, he eventually reached the city, in the year 1903.

OVERCOMES THE HOSTILITY OF THE BRAHMANS

As had been expected, Dharma Vijaya met at the beginning with the most strenuous opposition. It was not easy to overcome the hostility of the pious Hindus of the place, who would give the new-comers no quarter and no rest. Even those who knew very little or nothing about the Jain religion considered them as pernicious heretics, called them *Mlechchhas* (म्लेच्छ) and *Nāstikas* (नास्तिक) or unbelievers, and treated them as untouchables and outcasts. Undeterred by the difficulties which he had to encounter, and undaunted by the hostility of the Brahmans, Dharma Vijaya visited with his monks the most frequented places of the sacred city,—the recognized seat of the *Vedic* cult—and, evening after evening, preached to the people, explaining to them the fundamental principles of the Jain religion, not with a view to conversion, but with a view to making those principles known to them, so that they might correct their erroneous beliefs and ideas. Overcoming their suspicions and unreasonable hostility, which had its root in superstition and ignorance rather than in knowledge and wisdom, and which was oftentimes dictated by misunderstanding and misrepresentation rather than by hatred and malevolence, he at last succeeded in winning their good-will and their sympathies. A large building suitable for a college was soon purchased for the *Yashovijaya Jaina Pāthashālā*, which was now established on a firmer and sounder basis than before. The College, which admitted students of all castes and creeds, rapidly prospered. The number of students immediately increased. These students devoted themselves to the study of Jain literature and philosophy. Besides learning Sanskrit, they learnt Prākrit, the language of the Jain sacred books—the language which had long been neglected as a language, and almost forgotten.

HEMACHANDRĀCHĀRYA JAINA PUSTAKĀLAYA

Two years later a library under the name of *Hemachandrāchārya Jaina Pustakālaya* was founded and added to the College, which thus afforded additional facilities to the students. The library contains a rare collection of ancient and modern works, written in English, Gujarati, Hindi, and Sanskrit. It was placed under the kind care and supervision of the learned *Upādhyāya* Shrī Indra Vijaya, the first and the ablest disciple of the *Āchārya*. The College has flourished ever since under the able guidance of Dharma Vijaya, whose life in Benares has been, as it is always and everywhere else, an example of usefulness, self-devotion, and self-sacrifice.

F

VIII

THE MONK AT THE COURT OF THE MAHĀRĀJA OF BENARES

THE fame and reputation of Dharma Vijaya now rapidly spread in Benares. His learning and eloquence attracted more and more hearers every day. People came from distant parts of the city to hear his sermons. He soon became the talk of the city; and the subjects of his discourses began to be discussed by men of all creeds, even by the Pandits versed in the *Vedas*. One day, the Mahārāja of Benares sent for him, and the humble and unpretentious *Sādhu* accepted the invitation. The significance of that honour consisted, not in the fact that it was conferred on himself, but in that it was conferred on a *Jain* monk by a Mahārāja who was himself a very orthodox *Hindu*, and a strong champion of the *Hindu* faith. Dharma Vijaya went to the palace with his monks, and there, in the presence of the Mahārāja and the learned Pandits of his court, delivered a sermon which had for its subject the following verse:—

पञ्चैतानि पवित्राणि सर्वेषां धर्मचारिणाम् ।
अहिंसा सत्यमस्तेयं त्यागो मैथुनवर्जनम् ॥ १ ॥

'*These five are sacred for all religious men: Non-injury, Truthfulness, Non-stealing, Renunciation and Celibacy.*'

JAINISM NOT AN ATHEISM

He began by saying that Jainism, which hitherto has been frequently misrepresented and much misunderstood, is not in any sense an Atheism, the religion of Atheists or unbelievers, who disbelieve the existence of God, and who regard soul as nothing but an outcome of a particular combination of atoms of matter. He pointed out explicitly, and in an expressive and unambiguous manner, that the Jain religion did not deny the existence of God, the Supreme Being, the *Paramātman*. He stated in clear and emphatic terms that to call Jainism or the religion of the Jainas,—the religion which affirms the existence of, and teaches obedience to, God, the Paramount Power; the religion which maintains the immortality of the soul and its growth; the religion which distinguishes *Punya*, or good, which is the cause of happiness, from *Pāpa*, or evil, which is the cause of unhappiness; the religion which believes in *Moksha*, or final emancipation, the liberation of the Spirit from the bondage of matter, and demands the destruction of the *Karmic* bonds for the attainment of the same; the religion which prescribes the ways and means by which this salvation is to be attained, laying down the threefold path, which consists in Right Belief or Right Faith, Right Knowledge and Right Conduct—to call and represent such a religion as an Atheistic religion is manifestly absurd, grotesque and preposterous. Such a presentment is evidently irrational and unmeaning, and utterly unworthy of intellectual apprehension.

THE FIVE CARDINAL PRECEPTS OF JAINISM

He then made a lucid exposition of the Jain religion, showing how the five cardinal precepts of Jainism—*Ahiṃsā* or Non-killing, *Satya* or Truthfulness, *Asteya* or Non-stealing, *Brahmacharya* or Celibacy, and *Aparigraha*, which means freedom from greed, are the same as those in which the Hindus themselves believe. He explained that the general principles underlying all great religions are the same, and that Jainism does not teach anything repugnant to the religious susceptibility of the Hindus or the people of any other faith, nor does it teach anything subversive. The fundamental unity of all great religions was thus made apparent. He concluded by saying that a true brotherhood of religions can only be secured by members of each recognizing and honouring the truths contained in other faiths. The Pandits listened most attentively and sympathetically to the exposition of his faith, and eventually came to recognize that *it* also was a great religion, and, in matters essential, was not really alien from *Hinduism*. The Mahārāja was so much pleased with the simplicity, eloquence and learning of the Monk that henceforth he regarded him as a great acquisition to his State ; and from that day he began to take a keen interest in the *Pāthashālā* and encouraged its growth by all sympathetic means.

IX

THE SANĀTANA DHARMA MAHĀSABHĀ
AT ALLAHABAD

AND

THE PILGRIMAGE TO THE JAIN TĪRTHAS
OF BIHĀR

JAIN RELIGION AS TAUGHT BY THE TĪRTHAṄKARAS

In the year 1906 Dharma Vijaya went to Allahabad, whither he had been invited, along with other eminent and distinguished savants, to attend the *Sanātana Dharma Mahāsabhā*. This call afforded him an opportunity to speak of the religion of the Jainas in the presence of a galaxy of erudite scholars who had assembled there from all parts of India. In this splendid assemblage of the learned he delivered a lecture on the subject of *Unity*, which created a lasting impression, and proved a message of peace to the hearts of his hearers. He spoke about the Jain religion as taught and preached by the *Tīrthaṅkaras*, —the religion which endows everything observable with a living soul, giving extreme sanctity to life in any form, the religion which enjoins purity of life and conduct, respect and reverence to all individuals, toleration and liberality even to the unpopular and intolerant, and compassion and kindness even to animals. He spoke about his own faith; but in doing

so he sought to convert none, but tried to understand
all; and, in offering to share the knowledge with
which he was intrusted, he hoped to deepen every
man's faith by adding to it reason and knowledge, by
unveiling the common foundation which supports all
religions.

THE MONK AND THE MAHĀRĀJA OF DARBHANGA

The Mahārāja of Darbhanga, who was present, was
so much struck with the Monk's learning and eloquence that he invited him to his place of residence
and asked him questions about Jainism and Buddhism.
Dharma Vijaya explained to the Mahārāja the points
of difference, and proved to his satisfaction that
Jainism was older than, and independent of, Buddhism.

MAGADHA—THE MODERN BIHĀR

Dharma Vijaya now contemplated a resumption of
his peregrinations, in order to preach and scatter the
peaceful evangel of the Jina in other places. He had
before his mind the vision of the great *Āchāryas* who
had crossed the plains of Hindustan in all directions
to preach and propagate their religion. He thought
of Magadha, the modern Bihār,—the country sacred
in history as the land of Lord Mahāvīra's birth and of
his renunciation, the scene of his activities, the place
where he preached and attained omniscience and
Moksha—the country in which, except a few places
of antiquarian interest, nothing now remains to
record the ancient faith. Before the end of the year

1906 Dharma Vijaya left Benares with four monks and twenty students from the *Pāthashālā*; and, making his way through Arrah and Patna, where he was joined by several other students of the College, he made the pilgrimage to the Jain *Tīrthas* of Bihār, Pāvāpurī, Kundanpur, Rājagriha, Gunāyān, Kshatriya-kund and Sammeta-shikhara or Pārshvanātha Hill, which is considered one of the most sacred of all the *Tīrthas*, the place where twenty out of the twenty-four *Tīrthankaras* are believed to have attained *Nirvāṇa*.

X

MISSION IN BENGAL

AHIṀSĀ IN JAINISM

HAVING made the pilgrimage to the places sanctified by the Life of Lord Mahāvīra, Dharma Vijaya proceeded towards Bengal, the province where, he thought, the precept of *Ahiṃsā* was most disregarded. This precept of *Ahiṃsā* is considered the foundation principle of the Jain religion, so much so that the Jainas even call their faith '*Ahiṃsā Dharma*', the Religion of Non-killing. To them *Hiṃsā*, or killing, is the greatest sin and *Ahiṃsā*, or abstaining from killing, the most binding moral duty. According to them *Ahiṃsā* is the highest religion, there is no religion greater than *Ahiṃsā*.

VEDIC SACRIFICES

The doctrine of *Ahiṃsā*, or non-injury to all living beings, men and animals, seems to have found expression in a mystic and obscure passage in the *Chhāndogya Upanishad*,—one of the most mystical of all the *Upanishads*, where five ethical qualities, one being *Ahiṃsā*, are said to be equivalent to a part of the sacrifice of which the whole life of man is made an epitome. If we, however, examine the real state of things prevailing at the time when Lord Mahāvīra was born, if we consider the state of Hinduism at the time of the advent of this great *Guru*, we shall find that in those days *Vedic* sacrifices constituted mainly the creed of Hinduism. Animal sacrifices and oblations were the order of the day. The householders were under the direct control of a hierarchy of priests who, under all circumstances, officiated and propitiated the gods. These priests were, at all times, the mediators between gods and men, and sacrifices and rituals and ceremonies of all sorts and descriptions were formulated by them, with an eye to their own material gain. There was the sacrifice of the lamb, the sacrifice of the goat, the sacrifice of the horse and of all other things imaginable. Various were the reasons assigned, and various were the devices adopted for these dreadful and horrible sacrifices. In short, the sacrifice of animals in expectation of rewards in this world as well as in the other had become a world-wide institution.

THE ADVENT OF MAHĀVĪRA AND BUDDHA

Fortunately, with the advent of Lord Mahāvīra and of Lord Buddha a reaction against this institution of animal-sacrifice set in. Both these Masters of Compassion thought that such a mechanical religion of over-formal ceremonialism and life-taking sacrifices achieved nothing more than merely to cause unnecessary and unjustifiable injury to innocent animal life. They felt that such a religion could not purify a man's life,

G

could not satisfy the deep spiritual longings of his heart. They, therefore, made the non-injury doctrine a leading tenet of their schools. The spread of their faiths meant the practical abolition of sacrifices. The desire for inner religious improvement soon began to grow and made itself more and more manifest. The opponents of animal sacrifices were not only to be found among the Kshatriyas, but the more thoughtful and religious among the Brahmans also began to sing the praises of divine contemplation and practical moral virtues, and experienced the utility and usefulness of these, as against the extravagances of those cruel and meaningless sacrifices. The prohibition of bloodshed in connexion with all kinds of sacrifices is, therefore, a reform of no small consequence, for which human society might truly feel grateful to these *Gurus*.

RESPECT FOR ANIMAL LIFE ENJOINED BY THE SHĀSTRAS

For ages prior to Christianity the religion of the Jina not only forbade its followers to kill animals, but it also enjoined the strictest respect and reverence for all forms of animal life. To take any life, to injure any life in any shape or form, is to the Jainas the most heinous of all crimes. No wonder, then, that Dharma Vijaya should regard this precept of *Ahiṃsā* as of universal value, and should wish to see it observed by men of all creeds and countries. As soon as he reached Calcutta, he began delivering his sermons in the *Jaina Vidyāshālā*. He preached to the Bengalis, made them familiar with the noble precept of the Jain religion, proved convincingly by authority and argument that respect for animal life was enjoined even by the Brahmanical *shāstras*, and eventually had the satisfaction of knowing that at least some of them renounced the eating of the forbidden food.

XI

CONSECRATION OF MONKS

NATURE OF HAPPINESS EXPLAINED

THE next incident of importance in Calcutta was the consecration of new monks. Five students from amongst those who had followed Dharma Vijaya from Benares manifested to him their desire to be initiated as monks. Convinced of their sincerity and seriousness, Dharma Vijaya acquiesced and consented to favour their long cherished desire. Arrangements were made to celebrate the event, and, to add to the gravity of the occasion, Dharma Vijaya gave a sermon which had for its subject the following verse:

न चेन्द्रस्य सुखं किश्चित्र सुखं चक्रवर्तिनः ।
सुखमस्ति विरक्तस्य मुनेरेकान्तजीविनः ॥ १ ॥

' *Neither for Indra nor for an Emperor is there the least happiness.* (But) *there is happiness for a Muni, living alone and in detachment.*'

PERFECT HAPPINESS THE NATURE OF THE SOUL

He explained the nature of happiness, for which all men are athirst. There are certain things which all men desire. These things are health and wealth, ease and comfort, strength and influence, honour and fame, power and authority, freedom from opposition and freedom from pain. But all these things, all these objects of worldly enjoyment, however much they might gratify the senses for the time being, do not and will not satisfy the soul. This earthly pleasure, this pleasure of the senses, is essentially transient, imperfect, and impermanent, depending on contact with other things and bodies, involving pain and struggle for its attainment, creating worry and uneasiness after its experience, and oftentimes ending in altercation and strife with those who happen to be engaged in the pursuit of the same objects of the senses. What the soul wants is the real happiness, perfect, undying, unabating, and eternal happiness. This perfect happiness, this everlasting happiness, this ecstatic delight or bliss, which is neither the source of sorrow nor the source of pain, is really the nature of the soul, though man is through ignorance unaware of the fact. What prevents the soul from the enjoyment of its natural joy and its natural peace is ignorance. Remove this ignorance then, the ignorance which is the obstacle between the soul and its happiness, and learn to distinguish the real happiness from the unreal, the perfect from the imperfect, the undying and the eternal from the fleeting and the transitory.

BEHOLD THE GLORY OF THE SELF

Cast aside everything that is changing, everything that is unreal, false and fleeting. Through the outer form look to the life within ; through the outer vehicle look to the true Self within. In friends and in foes, in each and every thing around, in all circumstances

and at all times, through that which appears to the
eye look to that which the Spirit knows and feels.
Build on the real, the true, the permanent and the
eternal, wherein alone can be found peace, perfect
peace and perfect happiness, amid earthly troubles and
earthly sorrows.   Not in the continuous and constant
struggles of outer life can peace be found, but in the
heart of peace which abides in the Eternal.   For
remember that it is written that the path of realization is the path of the conquered senses, of the
conquered mind, when in the 'quietude of the senses
and the tranquillity of the mind, the man beholds the
glory of the Self'.

Thus preaching on the superiority of the religious
over the lay life, Dharma Vijaya made the aspirants
pass through the necessary formalities, and consecrated
them as monks.   This was in the year 1907.   Among
the newly consecrated were also the learned Muni
Vidyā Vijaya and Muni Nyāya Vijaya, both of whom
are scholars of great ability and have written several
works in connexion with the Jain religion and literature.   Three years after his consecration as a monk the
learned Muni Vidyā Vijaya wrote the life of the *Guru*
in Gujarati.   Recently he has also published in Hindi
a book entitled *Ādarsha Sādhu*, wherein he has given
a detailed account of the life and work of the *Āchārya*.

XII

SHĀSTRAVISHĀRADA JAINĀCHĀRYA

AFTER the rains of the year 1907 Dharma Vijaya left Calcutta with his monks and visited Nadia,—the celebrated seat of the logicians. The Pandits of this place are well versed in logic and the *Nyāya Shāstra.* They discussed with the Jain Monk various topics of religious and philosophical interest, and had to acknowledge in the end the high degree of his learning and ability in those branches of knowledge.

THE JAIN SĀDHU HONOURED BY THE PANDITS OF BENARES

Making his way through Murshidabad, Baluchar, Azimganj, and Pāvāpurī, the place sanctified by the *Nirvāṇa* of Lord Mahāvīra, and delivering everywhere sermons and public lectures, Dharma Vijaya at last reached Benares, in the year 1908. The Pandits of the city took this opportunity of welcoming the Jain *Sādhu* in their midst. The fame of his learning and scholarship had already established itself. His greatness, like the greatness of other persons of his class, did not depend upon frail crutches, but rested on the solid foundation of the substantial work which he had done. His erudite lectures on the Hindu and Jain systems of philosophy and sociology had already elicited great admiration from the scholars and Pandits of Benares, Bengal, and other parts of India. In recognition of his uncommon learning in the *Shāstras*, of his educational and religious activities, and of his marvellous achievements, these Pandits resolved to confer on him the title of *Shāstravishārada Jaināchārya*. The most distinguished Pandits from all parts of the country assembled in the premises of the *Yashovijaya Jaina Pāthashālā*, under the presidency of His Highness the Mahārāja of Benares, and presented to him a welcome-address, conferring on him the title mentioned above, on the twenty-fifth day of August, 1908.

AN EXAMPLE OF BROAD-MINDEDNESS AND TOLERANCE

Dharma Vijaya set very little value on temporal honours ; nevertheless, in this particular instance, he most respectfully accepted the title, inasmuch as it came from the most learned and religious men of his own land. The value of the honour bestowed was immensely increased, in that it was conferred in the presence of His Highness the Mahārāja of Benares, who was a well-known patron of Hindu learning and an eminent defender of the Hindu faith. In reply to the addresses which were read before him on the occasion Dharma Vijaya emphasized the significance of that honour, not as being conferred on himself, as he modestly deemed he did not deserve it, but as being conferred on a *Jain Sādhu* by the consensus of the *Hindu Pandits* from all parts of India, and under the auspices of a Mahārāja who also was an orthodox

Hindu and a firm believer in the Hindu faith. Indifferent as he was to personal honours, he could not be indifferent to such a noble example of tolerance and broad-mindedness, which gave him particular pleasure, inasmuch as he also was a strong advocate of mutual tolerance and sympathy and co-operation. In consequence of the *Āchāryapada* bestowed on him Dharma Vijaya's name was changed to Vijaya Dharma, by reversing the two terms, as is often done in the case of Jain Āchāryas, and the appendage *Sūri* was added to it.

XIII

THE JAIN ĀCHĀRYA AND WESTERN SCHOLARS

INSTITUTIONS OF PUBLIC UTILITY IN BENARES, AGRA AND PALITANA

VIJAYA DHARMA SŪRI now thought of leaving Benares, in order to continue his beneficent mission of preaching and propagating the religion of the Jina in other places. Before he began his tour, he caused a *Pashushālā*, hospital for animals, to be founded in Benares, in order to relieve the sufferings of the poor dumb world. Towards the end of the year 1911 he left the city, accompanied by his monks, and proceeded towards Gujarat. Making his way through Ayodhya, Fyzabad, Lucknow, Cawnpore, Kanauj, Farrukhabad, Kayamganj and Firozabad, and, preaching in all these places the precept of *Ahiṃsā*, he reached Agra, before the rains of the year 1912. Here he spent the *Chaturmāsa*, the four months of the rainy season, caused a library to be opened and a free dispensary to be started, the funds for both the institutions having been provided by Sheth Laxmi Chanda, a wealthy and charitably disposed merchant of the place. It was also during this halt at Agra that he caused a *Gurukula*, an institution in the form of a boarding-school, to be opened at Palitana in Kathiawar, and called it the *Yashovijaya Jaina Gurukula*.

LITERARY CONFERENCE AT JODHPUR

Soon after the rains Vijaya Dharma Sūri left Agra, and, continuing his journey through Muttra, Brinda-bun, Bharatpur, Jaipur, Kishangarh, Ajmer and Beāwar, entered into southern Marwar. His presence there was taken advantage of by the Jainas of Rajpu-tana, who thought of holding a conference, with a view to bringing together upon a common platform Jain scholars and other workers in the field of Jain litera-ture, for the purpose of discussing and devising ways and means of preserving and propagating the various branches of their literature. The historic city of Jodhpur—the city which played so important a part in ancient and mediaeval times in the history of Raj-putana—was chosen for the seat of the conference. The first Jain Literary Conference was accordingly held under the distinguished auspices of Vijaya Dharma Sūri, on the third day of March, 1914. Several resolutions were passed in this Conference with regard to the steps which should be taken to preserve and divulge the productions of the ancient Jain civilization in that part of the country.

DR. HERMANN JACOBI AND THE JAIN MONK

It was also in this Conference, in the midst of a galaxy of erudite scholars, and in the presence of the most distinguished representatives of the Jain and other Indian communities, who had congregated in the august assemblage from Bombay, Bengal, and other parts of India, that Dr. Hermann Jacobi, the most distinguished scholar of Jainism and the world-renowned translator of the *Jaina Sūtras* from Prākrit into English for the series of the Sacred Books of the East, availed himself of the opportunity to thank the Jain Āchārya, on behalf of himself and other European scholars interested in the study of Jain literature, and show him their gratitude for his invaluable advice and suggestions to them from time to time, and for his constant readiness to help them with the loan of manuscripts and such other information as it would otherwise be impossible for them to procure in Europe. 'I may express', said Dr. Hermann Jacobi, 'the feelings of gratitude which for a long time I entertain for the distinguished Munirāj Dharma Vijaya Sūri, with whom I am connected through a correspondence of many years. It gives me great satisfaction publicly to thank him for the obligation under which his uninterrupted kindness not only to me, but also to other students of Jainism has laid us. He was always eager to give every elucidation on difficult points of Jain doctrine which were laid before him; and since I have been here I have consulted him on many subjects; he explained to me some knotty points in the *Karma-granthas* which had baffled me long; he pointed out to me the passages in the *Aṅgas* which refer to the worship of the idols of *Tīrthaṅkaras*, and assisted me in many more ways. By this means he has in a great measure contributed to bring about correct ideas about Jainism among the scholars of the West. We owe to him also the loan of manuscripts by which it has become possible to publish Jain texts. If he had not supplied me with manuscripts of the पउमचरिय and the समराइच्चकहा, I should never have been able to undertake the edition of these important texts.'

DR. TESSITORI VISITS THE MONK IN HIS SUR-ROUNDINGS

A few days after the Conference Vijaya Dharma Sūri left Jodhpur to resume his peregrinations, and, passing through several villages and towns, reached Shivganj, before he rainy season of the same year, 1914. Here came the learned Italian scholar, the late Dr. L. Tessitori, to pay his respects to the Jain Āchārya. The great simplicity of the Monk, his absolute renunciation and detachment from worldly objects, his learning and eloquence, his scholarship and piety made a deep impression upon the mind of the great Italian scholar, so much so that he was tempted to give a vivid description of his visit to the Jain Monk, in a treatise entitled 'A Jain Āchārya of the Present Day', wherein he has embodied his views of what he saw and thought of that great *Āchārya*. 'Though Vijaya Dharma Sūri ', writes Dr. Tessitori, ' is very well known to all Orientalists in Europe whose sphere of work is directly or indirectly associated with Jainism—and he reckons amongst his friends Dr. F. W. Thomas, Prof. H. Jacobi, Dr. J. Hertel, Dr. A. Guérinot, &c.—yet I am so far the only European who has had opportunities to know him intimately in his own surroundings. I have visited

him four times during the last three years, and every
time his extraordinary personality has aroused in me
more interest and admiration. I have known him as
a scholar, I have known him as an orator, I have known
him as a monk; and, though he is not permitted to yield
to feelings of worldly affection, I think I can say that
I have also known him as a friend. In the cells of
the *Upāshrayas* I have sat by his side listening to his
explanations of philological or philosophical difficulties
which had been puzzling me ; in the open halls of the
Dharmashālās I have listened to his sermons delivered
in Hindi or in Gujarati before a motionless and
ecstatic audience, and have admired his simple and
yet subtle and forcible eloquence ; in the temples
I have been taken by him right before the marble
idols and have read with him the Sanskrit inscriptions engraved on their basements. It is to him that
I am indebted for having had an insight into the
monastic life of the Jains which probably no European ever had before. At Shivganj I have seen him
pull out the hair of his chief disciple, Indra Vijaya
Upādhyāya ; in Udaipur I have seen him consecrate
two new monks ; in the *Dharmashālā* of Ranakpur,
where the evening dusk was fantastically lit up by
fires blazing in the courtyard, I have watched him
performing the *Pratikramaṇa* with his monks ; in
the stony forests of the Aravalli I have accompanied
him in his *Vihāras*, walking by his side in the middle
of the cluster of his white-clad disciples ; in Kathiawar
I have entered with him the village of Talaja amongst

the festoons, the flowers, the scattering of rice, and the *Jè Jè's* of the entire population, and have made with him the pilgrimage to the sanctuary on the top of the hill, without omitting to visit the ancient Buddhist caves which adorn the sides of the mountain.'

The rains over, Vijaya Dharma Sūri left Shivganj, proceeded with his monks towards Mewar, and thence, passing through almost all the villages and towns of Gujarat and Kathiawar, preaching everywhere, and causing schools and libraries and other institutions of public utility to be opened in those places where they were most needed, he at last reached Bombay on June 13, 1919.

XIV

JAINISM, ANCIENT AND MODERN. REVIVAL OF JAIN LEARNING AND CULTURE—THE END AND THE MEANS

STUDY OF JAINISM, ITS VALUE AND IMPORTANCE

By this time a broad design had entered into the mind of Vijaya Dharma Sūri; and, after having well matured it, he thought he must now proceed to put it into execution. Of the three hundred and fifteen millions of people inhabiting India only a million and a quarter to-day profess the Jain faith; yet, in spite of its numerical weakness, Jainism makes its own distinct appeal for a more informed acquaintance with its essential doctrines and tenets. As the students of religious history are well aware, numerous sects and numerous orders arose, new faiths and new beliefs came into existence, in that great province of Bihār, in the sixth century before Christ,—the century which in so many countries witnessed an earnest search and an earnest aspiration after higher truths and nobler lives. Mahāvīra and Buddha and Gosāla all then began propounding their own faiths, and besides these there were many other bold reformers who vied with them in establishing their separate organizations. Yet of all these different organizations, of all these innumerable ancient Orders, one only has survived in India down to the present day, and that one is Jainism. Here lies for the student of Comparative Religion the most attractive and the most fascinating problem of study. For, indeed, it is an interesting and an instructive study to find out and realize the true causes that have thus enabled Jainism to weather the storms that in India wrecked so many of the other faiths. Yet another reason that may well attract and engage the attention of the student of Indian Religions to the study of Jainism lies in the fact that a singular and an uncommon interest attaches to its history and its doctrines.

JAINISM NOT A SUB-SECT OF BUDDHISM

Within the last forty years a group of Western scholars, pre-eminent amongst whom are the late Professor Hofrat Bühler, Professor Leumann, Professor Weber, Professor Jacobi, Dr. Hoernle, Dr. Hertel and Dr. Guérinot, have effected a great advance in our knowledge of the Jain religion and literature. Many and very important additions to our knowledge of Jainism and its history have been made by these selfless scholars, devoted to learning and literature. For long it had been thought that Jainism was but a sub-sect of Buddhism; but that opinion—thanks to the labours and researches of European scholars interested in the study of Eastern languages and literature—has been finally relinquished, and Jainism is now admitted to be one of the most ancient and independent organizations of India.

VĪRA-TATTVA-PRAKĀSHAKA MANDALA

Curiously enough, to the general public in India Jainism—this most eminent faith—has become little more than a mere name, and even the most assiduous students of Indian Religions oftentimes fail to give it its due attention. In order to remedy this evil, and to supply the long-felt want, Vijaya Dharma Sūri has brought into existence in Bombay an Association called the *Vīra-Tattva-Prakāshaka-Mandala*, the object of which is to carry out work of a propagandist character on advanced lines, in order to further the cause of the faith of Lord Mahāvīra. In founding this institution Vijaya Dharma Sūri aims at spreading the light of Jainism throughout the length and breadth of India by the agency of trained preachers, who shall devote themselves to the service of the religion with a true missionary spirit. The importance of this Association can hardly be exaggerated. Not only will it afford Jain scholars and other students interested in the study of Jain literature a common meeting-ground to discuss and devise the ways and means of reviving, promoting and disseminating the various branches of the Jain literature, but it will also lead to a scientific study of the literature, breeding a truly critical spirit as well as a spirit of research, which will enrich the literature itself and remove from the minds of scholars of other Indian communities many misconceptions regarding the Jainas and their faith. May this Association, under the distinguished auspices of the venerable sage, Vijaya Dharma Sūri, bring about the revival of Jain learning, and inaugurate a new era of progress and advancement of Jain culture, paving the way at the same time to the reconciliation between the *Shvetāmbaras* and the *Digambaras*, the two great sects of the Jain community.

XV

THE LIFE OF THE MONK AND ITS LESSONS

ATTACHMENT TO EARTHLY THINGS FATAL TO SPIRITUAL
PROGRESS

SUCH, briefly and most imperfectly sketched, is the
life of the great Monk, orderly and progressive, self-
restrained and dignified; the life that teaches man
comfort in sorrow, and acts as a messenger of peace
and harmony; the life that teaches him to train and
exalt his own nature, to purify his own thoughts and
elevate his own emotions; the life that teaches him
that attachment to the things of the earth is fatal to
progress in the life of the spirit; the life that teaches
him something of the spiritual truths underlying all
great religions of the world, and guides him not only
in his spiritual and intellectual life, but also in all his
relations with his fellow-men, in the life of the family,
of the community, and of the nation.

DISCRIMINATING BETWEEN THE REAL AND THE
UNREAL

Vexed with the world, and discerning the valueless-
ness of the transitory, he left everything that was
near and dear to him, and, going forth into the homeless state, far away from the din and turmoil of
modern busy life, far away from the busy haunts of
man, he began carrying out his researches in the

spiritual kingdom, trying to ascertain for himself and out of infinite compassion for humanity, whether all this talk about spirituality was an illusion, a self-hypnotism, or a deep intrinsic reality, original nature of man. As he alternates rapidly from joy to sorrow, from pleasure to pain, from peace to storm, he learns to see in these successive changes unreal and unsubstantial forms, and to recognize through all a steady and unchanging and incessant life. He learns that the weariness which took all the savour out of life was due to the disappointments constantly arising from his search for satisfaction in the unreal, when only the real can content and satisfy the soul. Discriminating in this way between the real and the unreal, growing indifferent to all external things, the ever-changing forms, and fixing his gaze on the permanent, the changeless reality that is ever present, and at last resting on that as his sure foundation, he crosses the threshold of the *Temple*.

FOLLOWING THE NOBLER AND THE HIGHER PATH

Taking the five celebrated vows laid down by Lord Mahāvīra as the only entrance through which a man can pass to the ascetic state, he becomes a monk, not in order that he may escape from the difficulties and troubles of earthly life, but in order that he may follow the nobler and the higher path, in order that he may follow the Great Ones who have made the pathway possible for humanity, in order that he may become the teacher, the instructor and the helper of mankind, giving back to the world at large that which he himself has received. With this end in view, he marches from place to place, calling nothing his own, nor possessing anything that belongs to the passing existence, preaching to the people the highest truths of spirituality,—the truths which he has realized and demonstrated by practical application in his own life—in order to help those truths to be made practical in the lives of others, for their temporal and spiritual well-being, happiness and advancement.

XVI

VIJAYA DHARMA SŪRI AS A MONK, A SCHOLAR AND A PREACHER

FULFILLING THE EXALTED MISSION

HOLDING and maintaining the religion as taught and preached by Lord Mahāvīra, Vijaya Dharma Sūri is endeavouring to raise it from its present degradation, ever seeking to give it back its lost knowledge, its lost powers. And what nobler work for the monk of to-day than to permeate his less-educated and less-enlightened brethren with the Ancient Wisdom? What nobler mission for the monk of the present day than to go forth after studying his own scriptures and teach the Ancient Learning with the authority and power that can only be wielded by one of the same faith with those whom he addresses? Known for his unrivalled knowledge of the *Jaina Sūtras*, the canonical texts of the Jain religion, Vijaya Dharma Sūri believes in the educational value and efficacy of the study of all religions, and is ever ready to learn and accept from them all that is good and true. He has shown the world how consistent are the teachings of Lord Mahāvīra with the noblest teachings of other faiths, with the essential truths of Religion, and how it is very largely owing to misconception and misrepresentation that His doctrines have come to be looked upon with so much of suspicion. Being himself a strong partisan of mutual tolerance and cooperation, he has been endeavouring, since the very day of his initiation as a monk, to bring about a better understanding, not only amongst the people of his own faith, but also between the Jains and peoples of other communities, castes and creeds, seeking earnestly to remove all sectarian disputes and differences, all religious controversies and religious antagonisms of the sundered faiths which almost divide between them the Eastern world.

AN ADMIRER OF WESTERN CRITICAL METHOD

As a scholar, Vijaya Dharma Sūri is a great admirer of the Western critical method. He admires the comparative and historic method of study, which for over fifty years has shown itself prominent in the West, and which still more recently has been making its influence felt in our own country. Notwithstanding this, while not despising the conclusions arrived at by the patient and admirable researches and investigations of European scholars, he unhesitatingly puts them aside where they conflict with important facts preserved in history, or in ancient documents and imperishable records carefully stored up and not wholly inaccessible. But the most remarkable of all his accomplishments are his broadmindedness, which is more like a Western scholar's than a Jain monk's, and his wonderful sympathy for all men, irrespective of their caste, creed or nationality. He has made the

literary treasures of his libraries accessible to Western
as well as Eastern scholars. He provides European
scholars interested in the study of the civilization and
especially of the literature of the Jainas with manuscripts and such other important and useful materials
as would otherwise be impossible for them to obtain
in Europe. The *Yashovijaya Jaina Pāthashālā* of
Benares and such other institutions founded and
established by him admit students without any distinction of caste or creed. The volumes of the *Yashovijaya Jaina Granthamālā* and other books written
and published by him and his disciples are freely sent
to all the important libraries, Jain and non-Jain, all
over the country.

BIGOTRY AND NARROW-MINDEDNESS DENOUNCED

The greatest triumph of the *Āchārya*, however,
consists in his having conquered and subjugated
bigotry and narrow-mindedness. Unlike the other
monks, who enclose themselves within the narrow
circle of their daily religious duties, and who refrain
from any intercourse with persons holding heterodox
opinions and beliefs, Vijaya Dharma Sūri extends his
broad sympathy to men of all communities, creeds and
faiths. Above all good and evil, absolutely free from
what we call hatred or repulsion, nothing repels him,
nothing drives him back. He is love and compassion
to everything, love and compassion to all. He spreads
round him, as it were, an embracing circle of sympathy
and compassion. All that come near him, all that

K

approach him, feel the influence of his divine compassion. The orthodox Pandits come, and they find
solace here; the heterodox religious reformers come,
and they find solace here; the agnostics, the atheists,
the sceptics, the materialists, and even the young
collegians come, and they find solace here; all find solace
and comfort in the inspiring word, in the spiritually
uplifting message of the great *Āchārya*. Hear his
words to the people, words breathing out that divine
compassion, which is the very birthmark of every
one who comes from that great brotherhood of *Sannyāsīs*,—the representatives and repositories of the
highest Indian spiritual culture—the *Sannyāsīs*, not
of the mere cloth, but of the heart. Again, listen to
his sermons and his discourses, and there you will get
his spirit, so different from that which is often shown
by those who bear the name. How different is his
method of teaching and preaching from the one which
is being commonly pursued by many other teachers
and preachers in India who, from vanity or baseless
pretensions to right or merit, begin by arrogating to
themselves the whole truth and nothing but the truth,
and leave, with a unique impartiality and an unparalleled fairness, to their hearers and opponents the
whole of the error and nothing but the error! As a
preacher and a propagandist, Vijaya Dharma Sūri
possesses a power of argumentation, persuasion and
conciliation, which is marvellous and unparalleled. If
any person's style is an index of his mind, the style
of Vijaya Dharma Sūri's is one. It has been said that

'the sublimest philosophy expresses itself in the simplest language'; and, if one wants the best illustration to prove it, he has simply to go for it to the *Āchārya*. Bewitching and marvellous and simple, it is at once the language of the child and the philosopher in one.

HIS DISCIPLES AND THEIR DISCIPLESHIP

Vijaya Dharma Sūri has surrounded himself with a number of intelligent, zealous and devout disciples. These disciples have imbibed and absorbed from their spiritual teacher and preceptor his broad and generous ideas, his charitable and benevolent views, his liberal and helpful thoughts and sentiments, his pure and noble enthusiasm, energy and earnestness. They are assisting the *Guru* in his noble and beneficent work of helping and uplifting humanity. These disciples are known for their learning, their piety, and their chastity; and their discipleship is shown not in external appearance, but in internal truth and renunciation, not in the outer garb that is worn, but in the inner life, in the knowledge, the purity and the devotion which alone, in fact, open the gateway of Initiation.

XVII

LITERARY ACTIVITY OF THE MONK AND ITS RESULTS

ORIGINAL WORKS WRITTEN AND PUBLISHED

LET us now turn to the services of Vijaya Dharma Sūri in the domain of literature and summarize the results of his literary activity. The first original work composed by him is the *Ahiṃsā-dig-darshana*, the work in which he has embodied his arguments to show that the non-killing of animals is enjoined even by the Brahmanical Shāstras. This was followed by the publication of several other original works, the most important amongst which are the *Brahmacharya-dig-darshana*, *Purushārtha-dig-darshana*, *Indriya-parājaya-dig-darshana*, *Ātma-unnati-dig-darshana*, the *Jaina-shikshā-dig-darshana*, and the *Jaina-tattva-dig-darshana*, which is a summary exposition of the Jain philosophy. These treatises were composed during his stay in Benares and Calcutta. Most of them are of a polemic nature, dealing with controversial matters, containing discussions and disputations on moral and religious subjects of great utility and importance. They are written mainly with the object of making the general public acquainted with the essential and fundamental principles and truths of the Jain religion. Each of these books has enjoyed a very wide circulation; and the fact that almost all of them have passed through several editions is in itself a proof of their great worth and popularity.

VIJAYA DHARMA SŪRI AS A PHILOLOGIST AND A CRITIC

The work, however, in which Vijaya Dharma Sūri first revealed himself as an able philologist and an efficient and erudite critic is his popular edition of the *Yoga-shāstra* of Hemachandra Āchārya, published in the Bibliotheca Indica. Hema Chandra Sūri, the great Āchārya who flourished in the twelfth century, is said to have written 35,000,000 *shlokas* on such varying, diverse and distinct subjects as religion, history, poetry, logic, grammar, &c. As he wrote chiefly in Sanskrit, his name is held in high esteem, not only by the Jainas, but also by the educated Hindus. So great were the power and influence wielded by him that he came to be regarded and recognized as the ' *Kalikāla Sarvajña,*' the Omniscient of the Kaliyuga. Several editions of his famous *Yoga-shāstra* have been published; but these were of very little use to the students who desired to follow the subject in its original as laid down by the author both with respect to the text and the commentary. The want of a critical edition of the text with the author's own commentary thereon was keenly felt by every one engaged in the teaching and study of it; and Vijaya Dharma Sūri supplied this long-felt want by publishing his edition, wherein he has displayed a sound erudition and a great mastery of his subject.

THE YASHOVIJAYA JAINA GRANTHAMĀLĀ

But the greatest and the most lasting monument which Vijaya Dharma Sūri will leave to posterity is a Series of Sanskrit and Prākrit works called the *Yashovijaya Jaina Granthamālā*. The Jain literature, which is one of the oldest literatures of India, is vast and varied, containing many valuable works on history, philosophy, poetry, grammar, lexicography, logic, rhetoric, astronomy and other sciences. For the purpose of rescuing from oblivion this old and extensive literature, and in order to make the same easily accessible and more intelligible to scholars,—Jain and non-Jain—Vijaya Dharma Sūri has taken upon himself, with the energy and earnestness that are his own, the publication of the most interesting and important of these works. The laborious task of bringing out authoritative and exhaustive editions of those old works which deserved to be made known began in the year 1904. Since then about seventy-five volumes have been published, which include works embracing a very large range of subjects, such as grammar, logic, history, chronology, poetry, &c. These volumes are freely distributed to all the important libraries, schools and colleges in India, as well as to the distinguished oriental societies in Europe, and the very favourable reception given to them both in the East and in the West speaks of their intrinsic value and their importance.

JAINA-SHĀSANA, DHARMA-DESHANĀ AND
DHARMĀBHYUDAYA

In the year 1911 a fortnightly paper called the
Jaina-Shāsana came to be published in Hindi and
Gujarati,— the result of Vijaya Dharma Sūri's noble
efforts in that direction. The paper aimed at spreading amongst the Jain community a better, a deeper
and a truer knowledge of their own faith. Vijaya
Dharma Sūri himself contributed to its columns
a series of articles in Gujarati under the title of
Dharma-Deshanā or religious instruction. These
articles were greatly appreciated by the people, so
much so that they were afterwards collected into
a separate volume bearing the same title. The book
may be aptly called a handy manual of Jainism,
laying before the reader an easy and popular exposition of the Jain faith. The text is divided into four
parts, which in their turn fall into a number of brief
chapters; and all these chapters are full of practical
information regarding the present state of Jainism.
In every page of the book the author shows himself
a keen observer of human nature, and his remarks on
the present spiritual condition of a certain portion of
his flock are at once pungent, fresh and vivifying.
Each page of the book is a standing monument of the
writer's skill in the subtlest reasonings; and the
frequent quotations of Sanskrit and Prākrit verses
with which the text is interspersed, as well as the
interesting anecdotes by which the exposition is

enlivened, greatly add to the value and attractiveness of the book.

Another monthly journal, called *Dharmābhyudaya*, has been started in Agra, the result of Vijaya Dharma Sūri's preaching in that place. It devotes itself to articles written in Hindi, Gujarati and English on literature, history, archaeology, art, and such other subjects of great utility and interest.

ARCHAEOLOGICAL AND HISTORICAL RESEARCHES

Since the last few years Vijaya Dharma Sūri has been showing phenomenal energy in archaeological and historical researches in connexion with Jainism, and has been collecting rich and valuable material, both manuscript and epigraphical, thus giving a new proof of his great versatility and talents. Some important results of his efforts in this direction have already appeared. One is a monograph bearing the title *Devakula-pāṭaka*, in which the author has given an interesting sketch of the history of Delwada, a small village in Mewar. The treatise contains the text of twenty-six inscriptions found on the images and amongst the ruins of the temples, and the decipherment of these inscriptions throws considerable light on the antiquities of the village. Another important publication of an historical character is a series of works called the *Aitihāsika Rāsa Saṃgraha*, the object of which is to publish such Jain *Rāsas* as appear to possess historical value.

XVIII

CONCLUSION—AN IDEAL MONK

MUCH is left untold, much is too briefly told, too poorly described, as the present is merely a feeble attempt at showing in outline only the life of the great Sage and the main features of his work. It was not proposed in these pages to describe and discuss the latter at anything like adequate length; for such a task must necessarily be left to much abler and better-equipped hands. All that was meant here was to present in a general way the eminent Monk and his great achievements, for the general reader's benefit. Enough has, however, been said to show that Vijaya Dharma Sūri, the great *Āchārya*, when he becomes better known, will most certainly be deemed entitled to a high place amongst the world's greatest thinkers, its reformers and its scholars. May these few pages help on a better understanding and a proper appreciation of the most noteworthy recluse, the eminent seer and the sage. For India, to its great misfortune, suffers to-day in the estimation of the world more through the latter's ignorance of the achievements of the heroes of Indian history than through the absence or the insignificance of such achievements.

INSTITUTION OF MONKS IN THE OLD DAYS OF ĀRYAN CIVILIZATION

Looking back to the India of the past, we find its perfect polity, its perfect spirituality, and we trace its gradual debasement, decline and degradation millennium after millennium. Glancing backward, we see the ancient Āryan civilization, originally divine in its nature, slowly and slowly going downward under the still unconquered lower nature of man, slowly and slowly degenerating under the still uncurbed, uncontrolled passions of humanity. Consider for a while the ancient Institution of Monks; see how it was meant to be used and utilized. In those good old days the *Monk* was meant to preach, instruct and advise. He was not to preach for money, he was not to preach for power and authority, he was not to preach for fame or popularity, he was not to instruct for anything that he got for himself; but he was to teach and instruct in fulfilment of his own duty, in fulfilment of his own *Dharma*. He was to teach in order that there might be a succession of teachers to help and guide the evolution of the race. He was to have knowledge not that he might keep and enjoy it for himself, but that he might in turn hand it on to others for their benefit and welfare. Thus nothing would be gained by him for himself, for his own happiness; but everything would be gained by him for the people, for the people's happiness. And in this way his duty would be discharged and his *Dharma* would be accomplished. There was the ideal of the *Monk*, an ideal that might be summed up as that of the soul approaching *Moksha* or liberation,—liberation from the bonds of imperfection, liberation from the thraldom of matter—which asked no longer the goods of the earth, which desired no longer for any gifts of wealth, or power, or fame, which aspired no longer after the pleasures of the body or the enjoyments of the flesh.

THE OLD IDEAL REALIZED

This was the old ideal of the *Monk*, which Vijaya Dharma Sūri had chosen for himself; this was the true old ideal which he had resolved to make the object of his life ; this ideal, and nothing less than this, was the goal which he had set himself to reach. Even in his early years he had realized what he ought to be, and he strove with precision to become that which he aspired to achieve. It was a deliberate self-training towards an aim that had been definitely recognized, a distinct and a positive building of the character towards a definite end, a carving in permanent material of a statue of which the mould had already been made. Seeing thoroughly the goal which was before him, and realizing thoroughly the magnitude of the task which lay before him, he set to work deliberately in order to reach the definite end, the definite goal. And this work, this building of the character, was not a thing of fits and starts, it was not a casual building and leaving off, it was not an effort in this direction one day and in another direction another day, it was not a running about seeking and searching for aims, it was not a turning about looking for a purpose; for the whole was designedly done, the purpose was recognized and the aim was known. In him there was no trace of wavering, no shadow of doubting. Slowly and slowly did he come to acquire wider knowledge; slowly and slowly did he come to understand that there was a better and a higher life, that there was a great scheme and that man was an important part of that scheme. Realizing this, and realizing the splendour and the glory of the plan, he immediately resolves to become an intelligent part of it; he resolves to take his place in it, not merely as a straw that is swept along by a storm, but rather as one who has understood and recognized his share in the mighty work that is being done.

A LONG AND LIVING SACRIFICE

As soon as he gains the glimpse of the real amid the fleeting, of the permanent amid the transitory, he leaves his parents and friends, he leaves his home and his native place, he leaves his pleasures and his comforts, and enters forthwith within the gateway of the glorious *Temple*, which shuts him out for ever from all earthly objects, from all the interests of the lower world, save that of *Service*; which separates him from all human desires, save as he works for the helping of the world, for the helping of Humanity. To him the law of sacrifice has now become the law of life, and he voluntarily associates himself with it, in order that he may perform his share of the glorious work of aiding and assisting the evolution of the race. And in this mighty *Temple* of sublime serenity and peacefulness does he stand performing his actions in a sacrificial way, asking for nothing, seeking for nothing, demanding no reward for himself, performing his actions as so many duties, performing them because they ought to be performed, and for no other reason. And, again, his is a joyful giving of everything that he possesses, a constant and a continuous pouring forth of everything, for the helping and joy of others, for the benefit and happiness of others, his whole life having now become one long and living sacrifice, the law of eternal seizing and grasping and holding having been changed into the law of eternal and endless giving and helping and assisting, the law of constant struggle for existence having been changed into the law of constant and continuous service and self-sacrifice, that being the true Law of Life.